Brian J. Smith as Brandon and Christopher Abbott as Justin in the Second Stage production of *Good Boys and True.*

GOOD BOYS AND TRUE

BY ROBERTO AGUIRRE-SACASA

★

★

DRAMATISTS
PLAY SERVICE
INC.

GOOD BOYS AND TRUE received its world premiere at the Steppenwolf Theatre Company (Martha Lavey, Artistic Director; David Hawkanson, Executive Director), in Chicago, Illinois, on December 21, 2007. It was directed by Pam MacKinnon; the set design was by Todd Rosenthal; the costume design was by Nan Cibula-Jenkins; the lighting design was by Ann Wrightson; the original music was by Rob Milburn; the sound design was by Michael Bodeen; the dramaturgy was by Edward Sobel; and the production stage manager was Christine D. Freeburg. The cast was as follows:

BRANDON HARDY .... Stephen Louis Grush
ELIZABETH HARDY .... Martha Lavey
RUSSELL SHEA .... John Procaccino
MADDY EMERSON .... Kelli Simpkins
JUSTIN SIMMONS .... Tim Rock
CHERYL MOODY .... Kelly O'Sullivan

GOOD BOYS AND TRUE received its New York premiere (in a revised form) at Second Stage Theatre (Carole Rothman, Artistic Director; Chris Burney, Associate Artistic Director; Ellen Richard, Executive Director) on May 19, 2008. It was directed by Scott Ellis; the set design was by Derek McLane; the costume design was by Tom Broaker; the lighting design was by Kenneth Posner; the sound design and original music were by Louis Flinn; and the production stage manager was Diane DiVita. The cast was as follows:

BRANDON HARDY .... Brian J. Smith
ELIZABETH HARDY .... J. Smith-Cameron
RUSSELL SHEA .... Lee Tergesen
MADDY EMERSON .... Kelley Overbey
JUSTIN SIMMONS .... Christopher Abbott
CHERYL MOODY .... Betty Gilpin

CHARACTERS

BRANDON HARDY, a seventeen-year-old senior at St. Joseph's Prep, plays football

ELIZABETH HARDY, his mother, a doctor in her forties

COACH RUSSELL SHEA, Brandon's football coach, a man in his late forties

MADDY EMERSON, Elizabeth's sister, a teacher in her thirties

JUSTIN SIMMONS, Brandon's best friend, also a senior at St. Joe's

CHERYL MOODY, seventeen years old, works at the mall

PLACE

A suburb of Washington, D.C.
Various locations around St. Joseph's Preparatory School for Boys.

TIME

Fall, 1988, three days in the lives of our characters.

GOOD BOYS AND TRUE

ACT ONE

Lights come up on seventeen-year-old Brandon Hardy, hand-some, wearing a navy blazer, khakis, and striped tie. He is talking to a tour group we don't see.

BRANDON. — We'll start the tour here, and I'll tell you a little bit about the school, and if anyone has any questions, I can maybe answer them, okay? *(He checks — it is okay — then dives in.)* Great, so … St. Joseph's was founded by the Jesuits in 1789, which means this year is its Bicentennial, so … *get ready to party! (Awkward beat.)* No, no, I'm kidding — Uh, the campus is one hundred and two acres (including yes, a golf course, these … *pastoral* hills all around us). In total, there are only four hundred and four students, so every-body gets personal attention from the teachers and counselors, and something like seventy-five percent of the senior class goes on to the Ivys. Or the — you know — *public* Ivys. *(Beat.)* The quad — here, where we're standing — from the chapel to the fieldhouse, is kind of like St. Joe's heart. All around it, there are athletic fields for lacrosse and soccer, a stadium for football, three tennis courts, a gym for wrestling and basketball, and two baseball diamonds. (You can also row crew, if you want, on the shimmering waters of the Potomac, but that's more intramurals.) All our teams are Division One, and we're the only private school in the DC area that's Division One; which explains, maybe, why most everyone plays at least one sport, and a lot of us are second- and third-generation players.

Also 'cause, you know, *mens sana in corpore sano.* "A sound mind in a sound body."

Personally, in my case, I'm on the football and basketball teams — like my dad was when he went to St. Joe's — and being on these teams has really, really enriched my experience these last few years. (I'm a senior, Class of 1989.) *(Beat. Brandon smiles.)* Uhm — so — any questions? Or should we keep going? *(The lights shift — and come up on Coach Russell Shea in his office, sitting at his desk. Trophies and pennants and sports equipment crowd the darkish room. Old photographs of sports teams from the past line the office's walls. On his desk: A videotape. Shea is a man in his late forties. He used to be in great shape, but he's let himself go a bit. Elizabeth Hardy, a well put-together woman in her forties, is there, as well. They are already in mid-conversation.)*

SHEA. — I appreciate this, Liz, I appreciate you coming in.

ELIZABETH. Well, thank you for changing the time, Russ. The hospital was truly a, a *horror* show, with this accident on the Beltway —

SHEA. I saw that.

ELIZABETH. Do you know…? This is the first time I've ever been inside this building. The *Haley* Athletic Center. *(Beat.)* That's new. When I was in school, at Garrison, we just called this the fieldhouse.

SHEA. The Haleys gave a Major Gift to — for the Bicentennial — to re-name the building.

ELIZABETH. Tom Haley did?

SHEA. Along with his sons, Kevin and Luke.

ELIZABETH. That's right, they're a whole dynasty. *(Beat.)* Well, in any case, I feel like I've been invited into the … inner circle. The sanctum-sanctorum.

SHEA. Actually, that would be the locker rooms, on the other side of the pool.

ELIZABETH. Is *that* what I'm smelling? Chlorine?

SHEA. Boys; you're smelling boys. *(Shea looks uncomfortable all of a sudden.)* Did you see Brandon practicing with the team outside?

ELIZABETH. I did, yes, lucky Number Forty-two —

SHEA. — just like Michael. *(Beat.)* Last week's game, he was talking about his big trip on that, that flying hospital?

ELIZABETH. It's been an epic process, all the preparations.

SHEA. How's that work, exactly?

ELIZABETH. Michael … heads a team of doctors and surgeons, and they fly around to … to developing countries —

SHEA. "On missions of mercy," he said. (Now I remember.) Those words.

ELIZABETH. That's right.

SHEA. "Doing good deeds" — those words, too. *(Beat.)* When's he due back?

ELIZABETH. In another week and a half.

SHEA. That's what I thought, that's why I couldn't wait — it's why I called you. *(He begins:)* We have a classroom here, upstairs, with a TV and a VCR in it, that we use to watch tapes of our games. This morning, I came in — was turning on some lights — and found two freshmen, in the classroom, looking … well, guilty as hell.

ELIZABETH. What were they doing?

SHEA. "Nothing," they said. Trying to get some "quiet studying" done before First Period.

ELIZABETH. *(Smiling.)* Oh, and that doesn't sound suspicious at all …

SHEA. I reminded them that the classroom was off-limits to anyone but the Varsity Players, they apologized profusely, then … fled. At which point, I discovered that although they'd turned the television off, the VCR was still playing … *(Points to it.)* that tape.

ELIZABETH. Not the latest football game I take it?

SHEA. Ah, no, it's a homemade video that shows two young people, a boy and a girl, doing — *performing* — very graphic sexual acts.

ELIZABETH. How, how graphic?

SHEA. Whatever you're imagining…?

ELIZABETH. Yes?

SHEA. That times three.

ELIZABETH. Ah — well — suddenly, I'm grateful for my lack of imagination.

SHEA. They both say things — the girl and the boy on the tape — but their voices are so muffled, you can't quite hear — make out — the words. But the boy, Lizzy … Looks like Brandon, when I reviewed the tape. *(Short pause, then:)*

ELIZABETH. Russell — *(Thinking: "This has to be a joke.")* Russ, you teach Brandon, you coach him. You've known our family for —

SHEA. Since Mikey and I were in high school together, but — *(Beat. He starts again.)* You can see the young woman clearly.

ELIZABETH. And it's Brandon's girlfriend?

SHEA. No, I know Erica. *(Shakes his head.)* No, this is someone else.

ELIZABETH. Performing these acts with a boy who "looks like"…?

SHEA. You can't see his face the way the tape was filmed, but it … *resembles* Brandon an awful lot, yes.

ELIZABETH. And did they…? Do you think this girl and this

boy — who (let me say this again) is *not* Brandon — taped them-selves deliberately? For their own pleasure or, or recreation?

SHEA. They don't *act* as though they're aware of the videotaping, no, but *someone* rigged the camera — put the tape in — set the timer. *(He shifts in his chair.)* There was some kind of *planning* involved, is what I mean. *(Beat.)* From the way the tape was shot, like I said, you can see the girl clearly — her face, her front — but not the young man's, not *his* face, so ...

ELIZABETH. ... so how can you say it's Brandon, then?

SHEA. Well, from his back, his build, his hair.

ELIZABETH. God, I ... I thought you were going to tell me Brandon was getting some kind of, I don't know, *award* ... When you asked me to come in? A commendation for ... athletic excel-lence or — and you wanted to tell me in person.

SHEA. Not — *(Shakes his head.)* not this time.

ELIZABETH. I feel I should leave — be outraged — out of loy-alty to Brandon.

SHEA. I understand that.

ELIZABETH. Or call a lawyer. *(Beat.)* Who knows about the tape, Russ? Does Father Lawton?

SHEA. Not yet. (I'm trying to keep this out of the headmaster's office, because —) Look, we all know, Brandon's a good kid.

ELIZABETH. The best.

SHEA. *(Agreeing, overlapping.)* The best — hey, he's my captain. *(Beat.)* I'm hoping we can contain this ourselves, off — off the radar.

ELIZABETH. We?

SHEA. Me, you, and Brandon. While minimizing the potential embarrassment to Brandon, and your family, and the girl's family.

ELIZABETH. And the girl.

SHEA. Of course — her, too. *(Beat.)* I haven't spoken to any of the boys yet, because —

ELIZABETH. — because if you do — (I'm getting this now) — it becomes "official," something you *would* have to tell Father Lawton about. But if this is all handled by us —

SHEA. — by *you*. By asking Brandon if it's him on the tape.

ELIZABETH. Jesus, Russ, couldn't it have been one of the boys you caught? In the room?

SHEA. They're thirteen; they're not at that *point* yet.

ELIZABETH. But Brandon is?

SHEA. Look for yourself and then tell me I'm wrong.

ELIZABETH. *(Overlapping "look for...?")* "Look for...?" *(Taking the tape from Russell.)* Alright ... Alright, I'll — watch it, and then I'll ask Brandon.

SHEA. If it is him, Liz —

ELIZABETH. It's not, there's *no way* —

SHEA. But if it is — if he admits it — then ... you need to make sure *that's* the only copy of the tape that exists.

ELIZABETH. Right.

SHEA. And then — it'll be a private matter. Something you, Michael, and I settle with Brandon.

ELIZABETH. And when he says it *isn't* him?

SHEA. You give me back the tape, you wipe your hands clean of this mess, and the St. Joe's machinery takes over. *(The lights change. Liz walks from Coach Shea's office — straight to the den of her house. She is joined by her sister Madeline — Maddy — who is in her thirties. Liz puts the tape in her VCR and the two women watch it for a few moments.)*

MADDY. Good God —

ELIZABETH. I know; right? *(She turns it off with the remote.)* When was the last time you *saw* something like that, Maddy?

MADDY. Tenth grade ... when Samantha Selby brought her older brother's *Hustler* magazines to school.

ELIZABETH. *(Remembering.)* Samantha Selby ... She *was* trouble; almost got you kicked out of Garrison.

MADDY. *I* almost got me kicked out of Garrison.

ELIZABETH. *(Allowing it.)* You were ... *restless* there, yes.

MADDY. How long does the whole thing last? (Restless? I was *miserable* there.)

ELIZABETH. About — not quite fifteen minutes. *(Beat.)* It gets ... more intense as it goes on.

MADDY. Well, it's no question that he's doing this without her consent or knowledge. Taping her? (I mean, not in my mind.) The way he, he *shifts* her around? Like lifting a, a mannequin? And pats her like that, like she's a *pet?*

ELIZABETH. I know. Russell didn't really *prepare* me for —

MADDY. *(Mildly outraged.)* God, and let me tell you: If this were happening at my school, and one of our teachers tried to handle it ... not even internally, *clandestinely,* and — and it came out that he or she *hadn't* reported it properly?

ELIZABETH. Let's not derail here, Madeline. Russ thinks the boy —

MADDY. The miscreant —

ELIZABETH. — that he — (yes, all right, the miscreant, the whatever you want to call him) — but Russell thinks that he looks like Brandon.

MADDY. Well, and he *does* — some, as much as you can see.

ELIZABETH. A body; *that's* what you see, a boy's back.

MADDY. And his *ass,* you see his ass pretty —

ELIZABETH. I'm *aware,* Madeline.

MADDY. No, but listen to what I'm saying: All these kids that play football now? (Brandon included?) They all look exactly the same. Unless they're black or Hispanic — and that's, what, *three* kids at St. Joe's? (God, I detest that place!) But they all work *out* the same way, they eat the same cafeteria food, they get the same haircuts, they all — they *blur,* Liz. So yes, that looks like your son — *(Quick beat.) But* it also looks like every other senior at St. Joe's.

ELIZABETH. That's ever so helpful, thank you.

MADDY. *(Quickly.)* Oh, you're asking me about Brandon's *character.* You're asking me to vouch for your son's *integrity.* Got it. In that case, no, Brandon would never, not under *any* circumstances —

ELIZABETH. *Thank you,* that's what I told Russ. *(Beat.)* I almost told him that for all we know, Brandon hasn't even started having sex yet.

MADDY. Elizabeth.

ELIZABETH. What? He has a girlfriend, but that doesn't necessarily mean —

MADDY. — Yes, Liz, it does. *(Beat.)* Trust me, your seventeen-year-old, football-playing, Sunny Delight-guzzling, Izod shirt-wearing son is having sex. *(Quick beat.)* Did you not read the copy of *Less Than Zero* I gave you?

ELIZABETH. Well … fine, but — *(Pointing to the dark television screen.)* I'm sorry, but he's not having *that* kind of sex —

MADDY. I don't know, Brandon is an over-achiever — *(Off another of Elizabeth's looks.)* I'm joking on the outside, horrified on the inside.

ELIZABETH. Whatever Brandon and Erica are doing in, in —

MADDY. Probably in your bed, whenever you and Michael are elsewhere —

ELIZABETH. *Maddy —*

MADDY. Sorry — God — Why do I do that?

ELIZABETH. The bottom line is: He's not videotaping himself having *any* kind of sex and then showing it to all his friends.

MADDY. No, the real bottom line is: Whoever's on the tape, we

10

can't let St. Joe's *not* punish them.

ELIZABETH. Thankfully, that's not for us to decide. That's the school's issue.

MADDY. Issue?

ELIZABETH. *Yes,* and — and Russell trusted me, and I'm not — I'm not violating that trust.

MADDY. Oh, you mean like how that girl was violated?

ELIZABETH. *(Beat.)* What I keep thinking about? If it's not Brandon —

MADDY. *Since* it's not Brandon —

ELIZABETH. — then it's one of his friends, maybe one of his best friends, maybe a boy I've had over for dinner. Do you know? *That* scares me. They scare me.

MADDY. Please, I spend ten hours a day with these nightmares. (Or more; Thomason stuck me with Spanish Club again, did I tell you?)

ELIZABETH. Repeatedly.

MADDY. And with rare exceptions, these are not profound, fully-formed human beings. (And I'm talking about the girls, too, they can be real — they can be *harpies,* Liz.) These are, generally speaking, shallow, insecure, destructive, *soulless* —

ELIZABETH. Not Brandon.

MADDY. No, because you and Michael are good parents. You're *involved.*

ELIZABETH. We try to be.

MADDY. No, you are. Every day, I deal with parents who don't know what *classes* their kids take, what *grade* they're in. You may not be Brandon's *buddy,* Liz — which I think is creepy, anyway, when parents are *too* chummy with their children — but you're involved.

ELIZABETH. I don't feel that right now. Right now, I feel like — that I'm, I'm withholding evidence.

MADDY. You kind of are. Speaking not as your sister, but as a *teacher* —

ELIZABETH. Oh, God, do you absolutely have to?

MADDY. What Russ did? I'm pretty sure that's a fireable offense.

ELIZABETH. He was trying to *help* — I'm convinced of that. Going far beyond the call of duty.

MADDY. Thank *God* for the St. Joe's mafia, for those "Old Boy" connections. *(Beat.)* Have you called Michael in — Ecuador or wherever he is?

ELIZABETH. El Salvador. (Ecuador?) I left him a message; he

11

hasn't called me back yet. *(From offstage, the sound of the front door opening and closing.)*

BRANDON. *(From offstage.)* Mom? Hey, Mom?

ELIZABETH. *(Calling.)* In here, honey, in the living room —

MADDY. Now as much as I'm *dying* to stay, I should probably go —

ELIZABETH. — yes, that would be helpful, I think. *(Beat.)* I'll call you later.

MADDY. Leave me a message, I'm going out with Craig. *(Madeline starts out of the living room, as Brandon — carrying an enormous sports bag — comes into it. They hug briefly.)*

BRANDON. Aunt Maddy, hey —

MADDY. Hey! *(Looking at him.)* Good God, are you possibly taller?

BRANDON. What?

MADDY. Since I last saw you, have you gotten taller?

BRANDON. Uh, you saw me two nights ago; we went to the movies.

MADDY. I'm sorry, but you're taller. Or broader. Which is good for me, because this weekend, you're coming over to move furniture.

BRANDON. I am?

MADDY. You are. I'm re-arranging my décor. I bought this amazing new piece of Outsider Art that must be hung ASAP.

BRANDON. Another one?

MADDY. Some people choose to have Children, other people choose to have Beautiful Things. *(As she goes, to Elizabeth:)* Call me! *(And then Madeline's gone, out the door.)*

BRANDON. That was — random. And — uh — what's "Outsider Art," anyway? She keeps using that term; I keep thinking I should know it …

ELIZABETH. Art created outside mainstream, institutionalized culture. Often by — *prison inmates,* isn't it? Or *wards of an insane asylum? (Brandon drops his bag, saunters over to the couch, sits down.)*

BRANDON. How was work?

ELIZABETH. — Fine.

BRANDON. I heard on the radio about, like, a fifteen-car nightmare pile-up on the Beltway — like, a bus crashed? — did you get anybody from that?

ELIZABETH. Several people, yes. All of them — all stabilizing, when I left the hospital.

BRANDON. Nobody died?

ELIZABETH. Not yet.

BRANDON. But — I mean — that's pretty *fortuitous,* right?

ELIZABETH. Extremely.

BRANDON. Okay, then — how come you look so *fraught,* mom?

ELIZABETH. I do? Fraught?

BRANDON. Yeah, you know: "Full of or accompanied by problems, dangers, or difficulties."

ELIZABETH. — right.

BRANDON. "Full of or expressing nervous tension and/or anxiety."

ELIZABETH. (You're never going to forgive us for that SAT Prep Course, are you?)

BRANDON. *(Jaunty.)* Hey, I *loved* that Kaplan class. I *loved* giving up my weekends for two whole months. I *loved* that my verbal score jumped a whole *twenty* points!

ELIZABETH. Son —

BRANDON. *(Sincerely.)* I'm kidding, Mom; I'm not that bitter. (Much.)

ELIZABETH. We — we talk, don't we? It's not just your father you tell things to — you trust — it's me, too?

BRANDON. I mean ... sure.

ELIZABETH. We look at how other kids are with their parents, the distance, the estrangement between them, and ... we're not like that, are we? We ... respect each other?

BRANDON. I respect you. *(Laying it on.)* And all adults.

ELIZABETH. There are no secrets — no *real* secrets — between us?

BRANDON. Mom — no — what's — ?

ELIZABETH. *(All in one breath.)* Brandon, you didn't videotape yourself having sex with some young woman and then bring the tape to school for whatever reason, did you?

BRANDON. I mean, WHAT?

ELIZABETH. Russell found a videotape of two students having sex.

BRANDON. The Coach did?

ELIZABETH. In the VCR your team uses to watch games, yes.

BRANDON. Jesus. And he thinks — ? *(Mini-beat.)* Wait, *you* think — ?

ELIZABETH. I don't think anything, I'm asking.

BRANDON. Why?

ELIZABETH. Frankly, it *does* look like you, honey. Your back, your shoulders, the back of your head.

BRANDON. Wait — hold on — you *saw* this sex tape?

ELIZABETH. Yes.

BRANDON. *(Shocked.)* On *our* VCR?!

ELIZABETH. Russell lent it to me.

BRANDON. *(More shocked.)* "*Lent* it to you!" Wait, are you *kidding?!* He gave this tape to you?!

ELIZABETH. Maddy couldn't believe it, either.

BRANDON. *Aunt* Maddy? Did *she* see it, too?

ELIZABETH. *(A beat — then, somewhat sheepishly:)* A few minutes of it ...

BRANDON. *Jesus Christ, Mom! (Beat.)* But — but the Coach *knows* me. He's like my —

ELIZABETH. I know; he knows.

BRANDON. You're my mom!

ELIZABETH. Well aware of that fact, honey, and if you let me finish —

BRANDON. You don't have to because it's not me, okay?

ELIZABETH. Well, of *course* not.

BRANDON. I mean, can't you just see that it's not me?

ELIZABETH. No, I was about to tell you. His face, the boy's face, is obscured.

BRANDON. Oh, so it could be *anyone,* then?

ELIZABETH. — yes.

BRANDON. I mean, it could be someone who doesn't even *go* to St. Joe's.

ELIZABETH. That's — *(Realizing.)* That's possible.

BRANDON. I mean, unless Coach Shea has some "insider information."

ELIZABETH. No. No, he was only trying to — to help us.

BRANDON. He threw me under the bus, mom!

ELIZABETH. He didn't, he just — *(Beat, reasoning it out.)* Tomorrow ... I'll give the tape back to Russ. I'll suggest that it might not even be someone from St. Joe's ...

BRANDON. Duh.

ELIZABETH. ... that maybe the tape just ... made its way to one of your classmates?

BRANDON. I mean, I hate to say it, but that's definitely a possibility. Some of the guys at school are into some pretty — no, some *seriously* crude shit. *(Beat.)* Jesus, I thought you were gonna, like, *confront* me about something else.

ELIZABETH. *(Big dread.)* Oh, God, what?

BRANDON. This seems anti-climactic now, and I was gonna wait until dad got back, but ...

ELIZABETH. What, Brandon?

BRANDON. I guess I got into Dartmouth.

ELIZABETH. You did? *(Confused.)* What?

BRANDON. Yeah. Early Decision.

ELIZABETH. When — honey, when did you find this out?

BRANDON. Last week. I got the call last — Tuesday. Letter to follow imminently, they said.

ELIZABETH. *(Thrilled.)* Brandon — honey —

BRANDON. Yeah, I'm pretty — *(Mini-beat.)* fairly pumped about it, Mom.

ELIZABETH. But why would that make me upset?

BRANDON. I don't know, you were just acting so *fraught.*

ELIZABETH. But this is *wonderful* news!

BRANDON. No, you're right, it's amazing.

ELIZABETH. Honey! *(She hugs her son.)* We — we have to celebrate! Are you hungry — have you eaten?

BRANDON. I did, yeah, with Erica. She's — coming over in a bit.

ELIZABETH. Brandon, I'm so incredibly proud of you! (Of course, it's not where I went —)

BRANDON. Barnard's a women's college, Mom —

ELIZABETH. Or where your dad went —

BRANDON. Thanks. Thanks for that —

ELIZABETH. Why didn't you tell us you were applying early decision? Does Dad know?

BRANDON. No, I was keeping it quiet.

ELIZABETH. We could've helped you. You don't have to — you shouldn't hide things like that from us. Even if you were feeling … pressure to apply other places, if Dartmouth's your first choice —

BRANDON. That, and Berkeley.

ELIZABETH. So far away? No, Dartmouth's better; we love Dartmouth, we love New Hampshire! Hanover, here we come! *(Beat.)* We have to call your dad, your grandparents …

BRANDON. Okay.

ELIZABETH. Brandon, this is so exciting! Hang on one second, will you? *(She starts out of the room.)* I'm getting my camera —

BRANDON. Mom —

ELIZABETH. I want to take a picture, I want to commemorate this —

BRANDON. Mom, it's not —

ELIZABETH. Wait right there!

BRANDON. *(Smiling.)* Of course. Absolutely. *(The lights shift, and — as soon as his mom disappears — Brandon goes back to the couch, picks up his sports bag, and walks to another part of the stage: The locker room at St. Joe's Prep, the next day. A bell rings. Brandon starts to change into his P.E. clothes as another student walks over to join him: his best friend Justin Simmons.)*

JUSTIN. Uh, hi, Brandon.

BRANDON. Oh, hey, Justin.

JUSTIN. What happened last night? I thought you were gonna call me.

BRANDON. Yeah, I was; sorry about that.

JUSTIN. I was actually *waiting* for your call, Brandon. (During which time, I finished this week's *and* next week's Cicero translations, which — before you even ask — yes, you can borrow.)

BRANDON. Sweet —

JUSTIN. I'd give you my AP Bio homework —

BRANDON. Dr. Justin Simmons, soon to be —

JUSTIN. But oh, that's right, we're not lab partners anymore. On top of which, I'm *pissed* at you!

BRANDON. My mom and I were talking —

JUSTIN. All night long?

BRANDON. Yeah, because — *(Mini-beat.)* Look, don't freak out but I told her, okay? About Dartmouth.

JUSTIN. You did?

BRANDON. Yeah, so — we had to, like, discuss it and stuff. Call my grandparents …

JUSTIN. Waitwaitwait: Weren't we gonna wait until *I* heard from Dartmouth and then tell our parents together?

BRANDON. Were we?

JUSTIN. It was kind of a pact, Brandon. We kind of vowed.

BRANDON. I told my mom about Dartmouth, Justin, to defuse the situation created by her asking me about the videotape. *(Short pause, then:)*

JUSTIN. *WHAT?*

BRANDON. Coach Shea gave it to her.

JUSTIN. *(Freaking out.)* Fuck! How did Shea — ?

BRANDON. He found it because some freshmen assholes left it in the VCR upstairs.

JUSTIN. Fuck! But I thought Mitchell had the tape.

BRANDON. Yeah, but this is *Mitchell*. Probably he made copies and, and started *selling* them.

JUSTIN. (Fucking idiot …)

BRANDON. Shea thought it was me, so he went to my mom because he and my dad are friends.

JUSTIN. But it *isn't* you on the tape —

BRANDON. Obviously —

JUSTIN. Okay, well, that's a relief, since it's not like we've talked about it, Brandon, and some people are saying it looks like you. Plus, no one's taken credit for it, which — if you examine the list of likely suspects (i.e. your troglodyte teammates) — is pretty uncharacteristic.

BRANDON. It looks like me, whatever, but it also looks like Miller, it also looks like Daniel, it also looks like — well, I mean, it sort of looks like you, too, stud.

JUSTIN. *(Big-time sarcastic.)* Oh, yeah, it was me, sorry, I forgot.

BRANDON. I'm just playing devil's advocate. *(Beat.)* Anyway, you were there with us, you *saw* the tape —

JUSTIN. I *left*, Brandon, as soon as I realized —

BRANDON. What do you want, a *medal? (Beat. Softer.)* You're not on the team with us, you had a choice.

JUSTIN. You're captain, you can do whatever you want.

BRANDON. Yeah, but I was, like … *transfixed*, okay? And … and it *did* feel wrong, watching the tape. But also … not *that* wrong. It was kind of …

JUSTIN. Stimulating?

BRANDON. Kind of.

JUSTIN. What, you, like … got a woodie?

BRANDON. A *what?* A *woodie?*

JUSTIN. Or whatever.

BRANDON. An *erection,* you mean?

JUSTIN. Yes.

BRANDON. I am *not* discussing my erections with you in public, Justin.

JUSTIN. Anyway, it can't be Trevor on the tape, he's got red hair; it can't be Ridgeway, he's not big enough

BRANDON. Maybe it's Mitchell? (And that's why he "found" it in his locker?)

JUSTIN. Possibly. *(Beat, he thinks about it.)* But why would Mitchell — ?

BRANDON. *I don't know. (Beat.)* Because he has no sense of, of *propriety.*

17

JUSTIN. If you know, and you're not telling me —

BRANDON. Look, it's stupid — it's lame — and ironically, it's probably not even someone who goes here. *(Beat.)* And my mom gave Coach Shea the tape back this morning, so it's not like it's an issue anymore, and — and we shouldn't *obsess* over it, and you shouldn't turn this into one of your — you know, things.

JUSTIN. Things?

BRANDON. Things you fixate on, Rain Man.

JUSTIN. — okay.

BRANDON. And I'm sorry. That I didn't call you last night. I meant to.

JUSTIN. I just … I fucking *hate* this place sometimes, you know? All the fucking columns, all the goddamn marble, it's *suffocating*.

BRANDON. It's *high school*, Justin. The Roman Empire fell over fifteen hundred years ago and we're *still* taking Latin.

JUSTIN. Hey, can we *please* not be on opposite teams today?

BRANDON. Uhm — we always are.

JUSTIN. Yeah, okay, fine, but just *once* can't we be teammates?

BRANDON. Nope, and how many times do I have to explain why? *(Beat.)* When we're on the same team — when we're both *sweating* and in close proximity to each other — I cannot keep my hands off your hard, hard body, and that makes everyone around us *incredibly* uncomfortable. *(Short pause as Justin looks at Brandon.)*

JUSTIN. Sick. You're a sick, sick bastard — *(A bell rings, signaling the start of the boys' next class — and the play's next scene. Brandon and Justin, now dressed for P.E., move to another part of the stage and stand shoulder-to-shoulder, as if they were in a line-up with their other classmates — which they are, we just don't see the classmates. Shea enters, blowing his whistle. He is standing in front of his class, talking to them.)*

SHEA. Two lines, gentlemen! Now before we divide into teams, there's something requiring our immediate attention. *(He dives in.)* Today, this morning, Father Lawton called me into his office and informed me that he had received several *distressing* phone calls from concerned parents. From the mothers and fathers of some of your fellow students, freshmen and sophomore boys. Who told them they had heard rumors about a videotape which showed one of their classmates … being intimate with a young woman. As well as about a screening of said videotape on school grounds. *(The two boys exchange a charged look.)* When Father Lawton asked me if I knew anything about these *distressing* accusations, I was *ashamed* to have to tell him

18

that I *did.* That I had, in fact, found and confiscated the tape, and that I was in the process of investigating the situation, which I will continue to do. *(Beat.)* Father Lawton has asked me to talk to the Junior and Senior classes and to ask anyone with any information about who made this tape — or who took part in this supposed screening — to step forward. *(Justin raises his hand, stands, whatever.)*

JUSTIN. Coach Shea?

SHEA. Mr. Simmons —

JUSTIN. Can't you just see who it is on the tape?

SHEA. Unfortunately, Mr. Simmons, we can't, no. *(Pointedly.)* Why do you ask?

JUSTIN. I'm a ... naturally curious person, I guess.

SHEA. Mr. Simmons — gentlemen — Father Lawton is so *perturbed* by these allegations, he has decided that until the person or persons involved step forward, you are *all* on probation. In other words: No extra-curriculars for any and all upper-classmen, and — *(The tiniest hitch in his voice.)* no sports. No practicing, no scrimmaging, no playing — *NO GAMES! (The boys react.)* Therefore, my *personal* advice to whomever participated in this affront? Step forward with whatever information you have — receive your punishment — and let the rest of us continue with our year and our season. *(Justin raises his hand again.)*

JUSTIN. Uh, me, again.

SHEA. *(Hating Justin.)* Simmons?

JUSTIN. What's so awful if you only *watched?* What's the big deal? I mean, it had already happened, so — so it's not like we could've *stopped* it, right?

SHEA. *(Really hating Justin.)* Mr. Simmons — would you mind telling me what St. Joseph's mission statement is?

JUSTIN. Uh ...

SHEA. Which you were asked — *(Takes in the entire class.)* which you were *all* asked — to commit to memory freshman year? Fifty push-ups for everyone if you *can't* tell me.

JUSTIN. Uhm ... *(Justin doesn't remember, so Brandon bails him out.)*

BRANDON. "To be good boys and true. To strive towards competence, courage, and compassion always. To become men of faith and to live as men for others."

JUSTIN. What he said.

SHEA. Correct. *(Beat.)* And the First Principle of Jesuit Spirituality, Mr. Hardy?

BRANDON. *Cura Personalis.*

SHEA. *Cura Personalis:* "The person in front of me is the most important person in the world." *(Beat.)* Fifty push-ups, gentlemen! *(He glares at Justin, and the boys start doing push-ups; as they do, Shea continues:)* What's so *awful,* Mr. Simmons, is that there is *nothing* courageous or compassionate about what was done to this young lady on that tape. It was a — a demeaning, shameful, and exploitative act involving some or many of you. And that, Mr. Simmons, you'll pardon my language, is the *big* fucking deal. *(The lights shift. A hallway at Elizabeth's hospital. Maddy is sitting on a chair, Elizabeth is standing; they are in mid-conversation. Maddy's agitated.)*

MADDY. Finally! What is the *point* of having a pager if you don't call people back?

ELIZABETH. I've been in surgery, Maddy.

MADDY. Liz — *(Dragging her to a corner of the stage.)* first thing this morning, Thomason summoned us into the lounge for an emergency meeting.

ELIZABETH. Why?

MADDY. A reporter from Channel Five called him to ask if he — or anyone on his staff — knew anything about a sex tape that's been making the rounds.

ELIZABETH. What did you say?

MADDY. I lied, of course; *that* made me feel like shit …

ELIZABETH. Was it the same one I — ?

MADDY. *(Sarcastic.)* No, Liz, it's a completely unrelated sex tape involving two other minors.

ELIZABETH. Well, *I* don't know.

MADDY. Thomason said — that this reporter said — that students at *four* different schools had seen or heard about the tape. And I asked my homeroom, and they *definitely* knew what I was talking about. A few of them — well, two, at least, Damien and Charles — had seen it.

ELIZABETH. Damien … the arsonist? And Charles … the kleptomaniac?

MADDY. They said that the boy on the tape is a football player at St. Joe's — that that's what they've heard.

ELIZABETH. "What they've heard"? So this is just gossip?

MADDY. Right now? Yes. But, maybe we were wrong, Liz. Maybe I was wrong. Maybe it was Brandon.

ELIZABETH. No, I asked him; he would've told me.

MADDY. OK, well what if it was one of his friends, like you said? Brandon could be protecting him. Which would make him, at a minimum, guilty by association.

ELIZABETH. (Fuck.) Alright, I'll call Russ, I'll call Michael again. *(Elizabeth is pulling a beeper out of her pocket, turns it on.)* Eight new pages?

MADDY. Four of those are from me — *(Super-annoyed again.)* (Check your pager!)

ELIZABETH. *(Checking.)* And one from Brandon —

MADDY. Here we go.

ELIZABETH. No, no, he always pages me after practice.

MADDY. — OK.

ELIZABETH. And three from — I think that's Russell's number. He paged me three — no, four times ... *(The two women look at each other. Oh, boy ...)*

MADDY. I tried telling you, when you and Michael were deciding where to send Brandon ...

ELIZABETH. *(Realizing what Maddy's getting at.)* Don't.

MADDY. *(Not angry yet, calmly.)* "Send him to me," I said, "Send him to Wilson, it's a public school, but he'll get an excellent education there."

ELIZABETH. Yes, except we actually wanted him to attend college.

MADDY. *(Starting to get angry.)* "Or — *or,* if it has to be a private school, at least send him somewhere co-ed."

ELIZABETH. Michael went to St. Joseph's, Maddy.

MADDY. *(Now angry, if desired.)* And you rolled over — you didn't object — you didn't even offer a dissenting opinion.

ELIZABETH. I couldn't; it's what Michael wanted, it's what Brandon wanted, it's what — it's what *I* wanted, too, and why not?

MADDY. People hate that school, Liz, not just me. Because that tape? Things like that tape happen at St. Joseph's — all — the — time. *(The lights shift. We're in Justin's bedroom with Brandon and Justin. Justin — who's electric in this scene — may be tossing a baseball in the air and catching it.)*

JUSTIN. Where did you meet?

BRANDON. The maintenance tunnels, under the Old Gym.

JUSTIN. Jocks meeting underground? In secret? Hot. Say the words "circle" and "jerk," and this turns into the Greatest Story *Ever.*

BRANDON. God, what is it with you and circle jerks?

JUSTIN. Oh, like you guys have *never* had one?

BRANDON. *We haven't.*

JUSTIN. *(What a tragedy.)* That is *such* a waste.

BRANDON. Uh, we have girlfriends, Justin. We have *outlets.* We're *not* sexually frustrated.

JUSTIN. Anyway —

BRANDON. — *Anyway,* all those steam pipes? I now get why Duffy makes the wrestling team train down there. Sweat was *pouring* off us.

JUSTIN. Hotter and hotter. Who met? It was…?

BRANDON. Most of the team: Me, Trevor, Fitz, Mitchell, Shreeves —

JUSTIN. Oh, awesome. All my favorites!

BRANDON. Okay, Justin.

JUSTIN. What, I hate those — those —

BRANDON. They're our friends.

JUSTIN. No, they're *your* friends. Who tolerate me 'cause *we're* friends, but secretly, they can't *stand* me —

BRANDON. That's not true —

JUSTIN. Brandon, they call me cocksucker —

BRANDON. Aw, come on —

JUSTIN. Which, on a purely descriptive level, *is* technically accurate — but only *one* cock at St. Joe's —

BRANDON. Justin —

JUSTIN. — and I hope the owner of that cock is not about to say something insensitive and/or vulgar, because (considering I've *never* asked for reciprocity) that would be pretty shitty.

BRANDON. That's … *(Shakes his head.)* You've only done that a few times.

JUSTIN. Hey, I'm not complaining, I'm just pointing out. *(Charged beat.)* And I don't hate them 'cause of what they call me, I hate them 'cause everything is so — 'Cause everything's already mapped out for them, 'cause they don't have any questions about who they are or what their lives are gonna be.

BRANDON. You can't say that, you can't *assume* —

JUSTIN. *Trevor* is applying Early Decision to Princeton. He's gonna get in, of course, because he's *legacy,* and he's gonna study Economics, probably spend a semester abroad, probably at the London School of Economics, then graduate, then get a job in New York, then go to business school, Columbia Business School, then — like — become a Master of the Universe. *(Beat.)* Agree or disagree?

22

BRANDON. — Agree.

JUSTIN. Mitchell, Mitchell's gonna go to ... oh, *Tulane* or Georgetown, because he really *is* an unintelligent person, and not even his dad — even though he's, like, Reagan's Foreign Affairs *Lackey* — will be able to get him into an Ivy League School —

BRANDON. Okay, Justin, I get —

JUSTIN. Shreeves, Shreeves will go to Stanford, where he'll scrape by — become an investment banker because "Greed is Good" — get married to some sorority girl he date-raped in college, but hey, who can remember, we were drinking so much? — breed these genetically superior *über*-children —

BRANDON. You know —

JUSTIN. — I can do this all night long.

BRANDON. Proving *what* exactly?

JUSTIN. That they get everything they want. That if they want something, they take it. Or it's given to them. Whether they deserve it or not. Like it's their — their *droit de seigneur.*

BRANDON. When you say "them," does that include me, too?

JUSTIN. Yeah, it does.

BRANDON. Well, does it include you? *(Quick beat.)* I mean, we *are* going to Dartmouth. (I got in, you're *gonna* get in ...) Does that mean you're — ?

JUSTIN. I'm not a Dartmouth legacy, Brandon, I'm earning that myself. *That's* what's different.

BRANDON. Rain Man — *(Brandon's had enough of this discussion, which is going nowhere.)* do you want to hear about our meeting or not?

JUSTIN. — yes.

BRANDON. OK.

JUSTIN. *(Sarcastic.)* — but only if you think you can *trust* me.

BRANDON. Goddammit —

JUSTIN. — fine. *(Beat.)* You, Trevor, Fitz, Mitchell, and Shreeves met in secret —

BRANDON. We met in *private* —

JUSTIN. — and *didn't* have a circle jerk.

BRANDON. Jesus, I hate you sometimes! *(Pushing forward.)* We met in *private* and came up with a strategy.

JUSTIN. A...?

BRANDON. Which is — essentially — to do nothing. *(A beat, then:)*

JUSTIN. *(Huge sarcasm.)* That's great; that's like New Coke; that's just a *genius idea* —

BRANDON. No, think about it: Coach Shea, Father Lawton — they can't do anything.

JUSTIN. They've suspended your practice indefinitely, Brandon.

BRANDON. Big deal — Lawton canceled practice? And no games this weekend? Uh, check a calendar, Father, no games were scheduled. (Convenient, right?) It's a bluff, they're bluffing. And when no one comes forward, when they see that their — their "scare tactics" aren't going to yield any results, they'll ... let it go.

JUSTIN. And — meanwhile — you guys do nothing?

BRANDON. *We tell the truth.* That Mitchell found the tape in his locker (which he did), and that we watched it, and that it was retarded of us, and that we should've known better, and that we should be punished, we should all receive two weeks of detention or whatever —

JUSTIN. Justice Under God —

BRANDON. Or maybe even one day's suspension — but since none of us *was* the guy on the tape —

JUSTIN. You know that for a fact?

BRANDON. They would've told me. *(Beat.)* And we asked around, and no one else is admitting to it.

JUSTIN. Not yet, anyway.

BRANDON. No, not ever. If it doesn't happen now, it's *never* gonna happen. Think about it: What Father Lawton and Coach Shea want is a scapegoat. That's what that whole speech in P.E. was about. Shea wanting us to get panicky — and turn on each other — and offer someone up —

JUSTIN. Yeah, like *Lord of the Flies*, Piggy's bloody head on a stake.

BRANDON. They don't want to suspend the whole team, they just want to *do the right thing.* And for them, that's punishing one person — then burying everything else. Agree or disagree?

JUSTIN. — agree.

BRANDON. Tomorrow morning, we're getting together before school — we're going to Coach Shea — we're admitting we saw the tape — we're apologizing for that — and then we're all gonna move on, slaps on the wrist, end of story.

JUSTIN. Yeah, no, your plan's ... *chilling* in its simplicity and brilliance, except that, you know, the girl on the tape is out there.

BRANDON. *She's* not gonna do anything.

JUSTIN. Maybe not her, but Lawton and Coach Shea —

BRANDON. — wouldn't be able to find her even if they *wanted* to,

24

and why would they? *(Shaking his head.)* No, they have to do a certain amount of digging because that's their *job,* but they don't — *(Beat.)* On a basic level, they don't *want* this to mushroom-cloud.

JUSTIN. Brandon ... you would tell me if it was you, right? You're not *not* telling me?

BRANDON. Again: For the millionth time: I know it looks like me, I know people —

JUSTIN. *(Interjecting.)* I'm not people!

BRANDON. — I know some of the *guys* are saying it's me, and acting like it's me, but I swear to you: It's not.

JUSTIN. Yeah, but — I would try to understand. I would help you.

BRANDON. Justin. Justin. *(Justin looks at his friend.)* It is not me, okay?

JUSTIN. ... okay.

BRANDON. So let's *vow* — let's make a *pact* — that we're never talking about that stupid fucking tape again, all right?

JUSTIN. All right, but — Dartmouth can't be like this, okay?

BRANDON. Like how?

JUSTIN. Like us being friends, but not at school... Like you being ashamed of our friendship.

BRANDON. *(Quick, almost angry.) What? Excuse me?*

JUSTIN. Not ashamed, that's not the right word —

BRANDON. Justin — *(Cocky, but believing it.) You know what I am, right?*

JUSTIN. (Oh, brother.) Of course, sure ...

BRANDON. I'm a goddamn *demi*-god —

JUSTIN. (Oh, Christ!)

BRANDON. And you're part of my *pantheon* —

JUSTIN. Oh, my fucking — ! *(Unsaid: " — Christ!")*

BRANDON. And no one — *nobody* at St. Joe's — makes me feel ashamed about *anything.*

JUSTIN. Yeah, Zeus, but we were talking about Dartmouth. We're gonna be roommates, right? That's still the plan?

BRANDON. Absolutely.

JUSTIN. I don't give two shits what those bastards on your team call me, but if I ever found out that you —

BRANDON. *(Definitively.)* I *don't* — I *wouldn't* — not *ever.* *(A beat, Justin regards Brandon, then:)*

JUSTIN. *In hoc spe vivo.*

BRANDON. "In this hope I live." *(The boys look at each other, the lights shift, and — Brandon crosses to his living room, where Elizabeth stands, waiting for him.)* Hey, sorry I'm late, I was at Justin's, he was having kind of a meltdown.

ELIZABETH. Brandon, wait, come here a minute. *(Brandon, on his way to kitchen, stops, returns.)* Do you remember when you were eight years old, you learned — *first* learned — to ride your bicycle? And how that summer, every day, you pedaled over to my friend Sarah Jordan's house?

BRANDON. Uh — vaguely.

ELIZABETH. She was older, she was sick — *extremely* sick, with cancer — and Sarah didn't have any children — and I told you it made me sad to think of her being alone — and so you started — you would pedal over to her house — and sit with her, by her bed — and hold her hand — and listen to stories about her life. Every day that summer, until she got so ill she couldn't be at home anymore.

BRANDON. Uh, if you say so …

ELIZABETH. I do. *(Beat.)* That's who you are to me, that's how I picture you, in my head, in my heart: A little boy holding a sick woman's hand. *(Beat.)* You didn't even know it was the kind, compassionate thing to do, you just — you just *did* it.

BRANDON. *(Laughing, this is all weird to him.)* Why are we talking about this, Mom?

ELIZABETH. Brandon, Russell just left.

BRANDON. He did? Coach was here?

ELIZABETH. He was. He … found the girl. *(Mini-beat.)* And please don't ask what girl, because you know who I'm talking about. *(Beat.)* And what you probably *don't* know because you're not *sweating*, you're not *shaking*, is that this is all about to — most certainly explode in the news.

BRANDON. What is?

ELIZABETH. The tape, Brandon. That it was made, that there are copies of it, that students at God knows how many schools have seen it.

BRANDON. *Other* schools…?

ELIZABETH. Yes, this is a lot bigger than it was a day ago, when we might — *might* — have been able to *staunch* the flow of blood. This is now something your Coach and I *can't* handle off, *off* the radar anymore. (Which I would've done, I *would've* tried to cover it up, to protect you, I would've done anything.) But now one of your classmates went to Russell —

BRANDON. Who did?

ELIZABETH. I have no idea — one of your teammates?

BRANDON. And told him what, exactly?

ELIZABETH. Where to find the girl, and — and Russ did, he tracked her down, and *she* told him it was you. And he came here to tell me it was you.

BRANDON. Come on, mom, not again —

ELIZABETH. *(Overlapping.)* I'm asking you, *again:* Is that you on that tape with that girl?

BRANDON. Mom — no.

ELIZABETH. Brandon. *(Deep breath, she starts.)* Not twenty minutes ago, Russell was standing right there — right where you are — was standing there and telling me that the girl on the tape, that the girl you — or someone who looks *exactly* like you because he *does,* Brandon —

BRANDON. Maybe, but it's not me.

ELIZABETH. And you wouldn't have *believed* the look on Russell's face. Or the look on mine while he was telling me.

BRANDON. I'm — seems like I'm getting a pretty good picture of it right now.

ELIZABETH. Do you know what I thought — what I was hanging on to, knuckles white, fingernails *shredding* my palms — while he was telling me? That my son is decent, a decent young man. That my son was raised to be considerate and thoughtful and kind and respectful.

BRANDON. I was — I am.

ELIZABETH. Fine. All right. *(Beat.)* Then if you tell me, again, that it's not you on that tape ... I will believe you. I will never question you again, I will stand by your side through whatever happens next —

BRANDON. Thanks, thank you.

ELIZABETH. But if it *is* you —

BRANDON. Jesus!

ELIZABETH. — then you have to tell me *that,* so it doesn't get any worse. (Because it will; it already has.) And I swear, I will do those same things. I will defend you, I will support you.

BRANDON. Mom —

ELIZABETH. The *truth,* Brandon. It *will* come out; it always does.

BRANDON. — it was me, Mom. *(Beat.)* That *is* me on the tape.

ELIZABETH. Brandon ... *(Pause. Elizabeth does something — looks or moves away — and then:)* why?

BRANDON. Why…?

ELIZABETH. *(Spiraling.)* … did you make the tape…? *Why* … did you bring it to school? *Why* … did you lie to me? *(Jumping on this.)* You *lied* to me!

BRANDON. I was going to tell you — when Coach found the tape, but I didn't want the girl to — to — *(Beat.)* But if *she's* telling everyone —

ELIZABETH. Who is she? The girl, the flesh-and-blood person you did this to?

BRANDON. Okay, but — are you mad?

ELIZABETH. *(Uh, "duh.")* Yes, yes, I would say that I am… I would even say that I'm *fraught. (Beat.)* What was her *name,* Brandon?

BRANDON. Cheryl, Cheryl … uhm …

ELIZABETH. … *Moody,* it's Cheryl Moody — Russ told me.

BRANDON. That's right, Moody.

ELIZABETH. And she goes to public school — Whitman, I think?

BRANDON. Mom — please — I — I didn't want to lie to you —

ELIZABETH. *No.* No, we're not *to* that part yet, Brandon. Right now, we're focusing on your other, even *more* morally reprehensible behavior. *(Beat.)* Does she — does Cheryl Moody — go to Whitman?

BRANDON. Yeah, I, I think …

ELIZABETH. You *think?*

BRANDON. We didn't talk a lot about school, I met her at Montgomery Mall. She works in the — in the food court.

ELIZABETH. And, and how long after you two met — how long did you know this girl — before…?

BRANDON. One day, that day.

ELIZABETH. *Pardon…?*

BRANDON. The day I met her — at the mall — that was the same day we — *I* made the tape.

ELIZABETH. The same…?

BRANDON. That afternoon, it was a — a Sunday afternoon. I drove over from St. Joe's, maybe — maybe three weeks ago, after Chapel.

ELIZABETH. And then took her *where?* I didn't recognize your room — or *my* room.

BRANDON. I did it at, at Trevor's house, in one of the rooms there.

ELIZABETH. With his knowledge?

BRANDON. No, he didn't know, he was — his family was staying at a hotel, down in Georgetown, 'cause their house was being renovated.

ELIZABETH. *(The horror of it.)* Brandon …

BRANDON. I would never have done it here, out of respect.

ELIZABETH. Out of *respect?* For whom?

BRANDON. I mean … for you, Mom.

ELIZABETH. For *me?* Brandon, if you had one *ounce* of respect for me — or anyone — you wouldn't have done this, you wouldn't have lied —

BRANDON. Mom — Mom, I am so sorry —

ELIZABETH. Are you? Correct me if I'm wrong, but not only did you make this tape — idiotic enough, forgive me — but you also brought it to school, demonstrating, to me, a pathological personality at work.

BRANDON. I — *(Allowing.)* I did bring it, yeah.

ELIZABETH. And organized a screening?

BRANDON. No, no, that was Mitchell.

ELIZABETH. How the hell did he get the tape?

BRANDON. I put it in his locker which he leaves unlocked 'cause … he can't remember his combination.

ELIZABETH. Oh, so we're dealing with a boy *genius* here.

BRANDON. He's a good guy.

ELIZABETH. Oh, *clearly.*

BRANDON. Mitch found the tape, took it home, watched it, brought it back to school, and then we all watched it together.

ELIZABETH. Everyone on the team?

BRANDON. Just about.

ELIZABETH. You *wanted* them to see the tape?

BRANDON. I … I don't know.

ELIZABETH. Well, you *must* have.

BRANDON. Okay, fine: Yes, I wanted them to see it.

ELIZABETH. Why? *Why* did you want them to see it? *(A beat, then:)*

BRANDON. Dad. We have to — You have to call Dad.

ELIZABETH. I did already. He's flying back — tomorrow — and a surgeon is flying out to replace him, and wait for *those* shockwaves, Mister.

BRANDON. He'll — Dad'll understand.

ELIZABETH. *(Outrage at this suggestion.)* You think so? You think he'll understand that three weeks ago, his son — his son who has *everything,* his son who is in the enviable position of being able to afford *whatever* future he wants for himself — that his son drove to a mall specifically looking for some poor girl, to, to *exploit?*

BRANDON. Don't say it that way, mom, don't —

ELIZABETH. What were you *thinking,* Brandon, while you were getting ready? Were you thinking: "I have to find a girl who's not that pretty, but pretty enough. Who will do certain things, things I'd *never* ask Erica to do. And not only must I do these things with her, I have to *prove* that I did them, so I either have to *convince* her — "

BRANDON. No, it wasn't about convincing —

ELIZABETH. No, that's right, there's no *way* you could have convinced the girl to let herself be — be *used* like that. Not even as charming as you are — as *handsome* as you are.

BRANDON. No one used anyone, mom —

ELIZABETH. Brandon, do you want me to get the tape back from Russ so we can watch it together? *(Silence from Brandon. She continues:)* Because this is what *I* saw, when *I* watched it ... I saw a boy — *I saw you* — lead that girl onto, what? Not even a bed, onto a *mattress,* on some floor... I saw her smiling at you because she didn't know what you were about to do ... (How *could* she?) I saw you turn her around — flip her onto her stomach — and ease her up onto her hands and knees ... I saw you grab her hair — and pull on it — and push into her harder and harder ... I saw you slap her. I saw you force her face into the mattress, so — why, so you wouldn't have to *hear* her? (What was she saying...?) I saw you — I couldn't see your face — but I swear, you were *enjoying* it, Brandon. *(Brandon looks at Elizabeth, not denying anything. Quick blackout.)*

End of Act One

ACT TWO

The lights rise on Cheryl Moody, seventeen years old, sitting at a table, finishing a soda, in Montgomery Mall's eatery. Brandon, in his blue blazer and striped tie, approaches her. We are in the past, it should be clear.

BRANDON. Hey. *(After a beat, Cheryl realizes he's talking to her.)*
CHERYL. Hi …
BRANDON. Are you working or are you — ?
CHERYL. — noI'monbreak. *(Beat. Forcing herself to slow it down.)* I'm on a break.
BRANDON. *(Gesturing to sit across from her.)* Cool. Would you mind…? Can I join you?
CHERYL. If you want — yeah — sure — *(He sits down next to her — a beat — he smiles.)*
BRANDON. My name's Brandon Hardy. (I should've said that first.)
CHERYL. Uh, it's okay. I know who you are.
BRANDON. You do?
CHERYL. Yeah, you go to St. Joe's, right?
BRANDON. Guilty.
CHERYL. And you're a senior — and captain of varsity football — and you also play basketball, and you start, but you're not captain.
BRANDON. Wow, that's — slightly disturbing. You're not — *stalking* me, are you? This isn't a *Fatal Attraction*-type thing is it?
CHERYL. Uhm. I know who you are and where you go to school, but I don't have a *shrine* built to you in my bedroom, so — *(Brandon does something flirty; takes a French fry off her plate, maybe.)* Me and my friends, we go to your home games, sometimes, so we've seen you play, and —
BRANDON. You come to our games?
CHERYL. With my friends, on occasion. *(Explaining.)* Whitman? Where I go to school? Doesn't have varsity sports.
BRANDON. Shit, that sucks.
CHERYL. For the guys, especially, yeah.

BRANDON. And for the girls, no cheerleaders.

CHERYL. Oh, yeah, that's a *huge* tragedy.

BRANDON. What, let me guess: You hate cheerleaders?

CHERYL. Truthfully…? I probably should — for what they represent — but … no, they're OK.

BRANDON. Cool, then you should cheer for us.

CHERYL. For the, uh — St. Joe's Knights?

BRANDON. Girls from all different schools are on the squad.

CHERYL. No, girls from all different *private* schools are on the squad — right?

BRANDON. I mean, I don't have the exact *break*down on me, but …

CHERYL. Also, I have this job — such as it is — so my schedule …

BRANDON. And maybe your boyfriend would get jealous if you were cheering for a bunch of St. Joe's meatheads? *(Beat. A shift in Cheryl's attitude.)*

CHERYL. See, I knew this was coming.

BRANDON. What?

CHERYL. This is a joke, right? You're making fun of me?

BRANDON. I'm not. (Making fun of you how?)

CHERYL. I *don't* have a boyfriend, OK?

BRANDON. OK, well — I didn't know that. I assumed, since you're …

CHERYL. What?

BRANDON. I don't know, I assumed … since you're pretty, that you would.

CHERYL. Pretty?

BRANDON. Oh, shit, is that bad? Calling someone pretty? Is that like calling someone cute? *(Quickly correcting himself.)* Hot. "I assumed, since you're hot, that you would."

CHERYL. You think I'm pretty?

BRANDON. Pretty — cute — hot — yes — completely. Else … I wouldn't have asked to join you, I wouldn't be asking you out.

CHERYL. Is — (Hang on.) — is *that* what's happening here?

BRANDON. … What did you *think* was happening?

CHERYL. I …

BRANDON. Do you want to do something — with me — tonight? *(Beat.)* I can *engrave* it, if that would help *sway* you.

CHERYL. Seriously? You're asking me to…?

BRANDON. Like, go to Chili's or something. I don't know how

late you work —

CHERYL. Six o'clock —

BRANDON. Cool, well … if you want, I can kill some time, go to the Izod store or wherever, and then meet you back here at six — if you want.

CHERYL. Sure — I mean — That'd be — Yes.

BRANDON. Okay, cool … *(As if he's suddenly remembering:)* Oh, we're gonna have to swing by my friend Trevor's house. He's away, his family's away, till Tuesday, but they asked me to go by and check on it; would that be okay?

CHERYL. Sure, of course.

BRANDON. Great, so … six o'clock?

CHERYL. I'll be here. *(He starts to go.)* Wait. *(He stops, turns back to him.)* I'm Cheryl, by the way, Cheryl Moody. *(The lights change. Brandon and Cheryl exit as Elizabeth crosses to a bench, outside the fieldhouse, on St. Joe's campus. She sits down, exhausted, as Maddy enters, carrying two cups of coffee.)*

ELIZABETH. *(Seeing the coffee.)* God, *please* tell me one of those is mine.

MADDY. One of these is yours. *(Handing her one.)* No milk, two sugars, courtesy of 7-11.

ELIZABETH. Thank you.

MADDY. What time's your *audience* with Shea?

ELIZABETH. Ten-fifteen. *(Maddy sits down next to her.)* Thanks for meeting me; your *skin's* probably crawling. *(Sips coffee.)* Oh, that's good.

MADDY. Are you kidding? Any chance to revisit our old *haunts* …

ELIZABETH. Oh, hardly.

MADDY. Uh, need I remind you? I wasn't a *regular* at the football games like you, but Samantha Selby and I *were* in the St. Joe's Players' production of *Guys and Dolls,* thank you very much.

ELIZABETH. That's *right,* I forgot.

MADDY. *(Looking around.)* And good God … this campus has not changed one *brick,* has it?

ELIZABETH. New names on the buildings, but otherwise … no. Which is the point, I think. *(Beat.)* Did you have fun?

MADDY. Doing *Guys and Dolls?*

ELIZABETH. In high school, at Garrison. Or did you *really* hate it?

MADDY. Every choice I've made since high school — going to Oberlin; majoring in Education; teaching at Wilson; the fact that

I only date guitar players — every choice has been a direct response *to* Garrison.

ELIZABETH. Right … *(Beat.)* God, and I *loved* it.

MADDY. Well, different strokes …

ELIZABETH. Yes, and — and I'm sure I didn't make it any easier for you.

MADDY. Oh, because I lived in your *shadow?* Because I was compared to you, *every* day, by every single teacher?

ELIZABETH. Is that what happened?

MADDY. Constantly, I was constantly being reminded: Elizabeth Emerson, top of her class … Most Likely to Succeed, Most Likely to Marry Well, Most Likely to Change the World …

ELIZABETH. I sound like a nightmare.

MADDY. No, Liz, you were … *fine,* actually. We were just … we *are* … very different people, is all. *(A long beat, then:)*

ELIZABETH. Brandon told me what he did, Maddy — the, the mechanics of it? — but he can't tell me why. I, I don't think he *knows* why.

MADDY. He has to.

ELIZABETH. He's seventeen. I can't account for half the things I did when I was seventeen; can you?

MADDY. This is not borrowing the school van without permission. This is not vandalism. This is not getting high in the bathroom.

ELIZABETH. I realize that.

MADDY. *(Suddenly.)* Listen, don't hate me but I told Thomason. Last night — late — I called him.

ELIZABETH. About Brandon? After we talked?

MADDY. He was going to find out, Liz, and I wanted to defuse … *(Beat.)* He suggested … I take a few days off. He's afraid people are going to start … making the connection.

ELIZABETH. Between you and Brandon?

MADDY. That would be the one, yeah —

ELIZABETH. That *bastard* —

MADDY. He *is* — usually — but this time … *(Beat.)* I *am* a teacher, and Brandon *is* my nephew, and a … a … *(Maddy stops herself. She's not going there.)*

ELIZABETH. Go ahead, call him whatever you want. I've run through them *all,* in my head, every name.

MADDY. *That's* healthy.

ELIZABETH. Thomason *can't* fire you —

MADDY. He didn't —

ELIZABETH. Or suspend you —

MADDY. He's not; it's my choice, he says — though it wasn't much of one: I *should*, at this moment, be teaching a Spanish 2 class.

ELIZABETH. Jesus, this has nothing to do with you!

MADDY. It's fine, *I'm* fine. *(Beat.)* And, you know, Thomason can go fuck himself. He wants to pay me to take a week off, fine.

ELIZABETH. You shouldn't have to.

MADDY. Except — if I don't, Liz, what do I say? How do I defend Brandon? To my students? When they ask me? 'Cause they will; they're *smart*.

ELIZABETH. They're soulless harpies, is what you said.

MADDY. Brandon didn't make this tape *with* Erica. He made it with a girl who could have been, just as easily, one of my students … Cheryl Moody doesn't go to Wilson, but I'm sure she's not much different from any of the girls I teach … And standing up in front of them, and knowing that your son — that my nephew — thinks she's worthless…? That he's allowed to…? *(Shaking her head.)* I can't. I can't *do* that. *(The lights shift. Maddy exits as Elizabeth crosses from the bench to Shea's office, where he sits, behind his desk.)*

SHEA. I — I feel sick to death about all this. That it's you dealing with this and not Michael.

ELIZABETH. He will be, very shortly.

SHEA. Well, we can wait for Mikey to meet with Father Lawton for the — the worst of it.

ELIZABETH. I'm his *mother*, Russ. I'm *here*, you can tell *me* the worst of it. *(Short pause, then:)*

SHEA. Pending further investigation, Brandon's suspended, of course, indefinitely. And … he's off the team. We're saying that's indefinite, too, but … it's permanent.

ELIZABETH. I — *(Tightly.)* imagined.

SHEA. That lawyer you mentioned last time? I'd get in touch with him.

ELIZABETH. Michael and I did, already. Jim Shannon — you know him, right? Class of — '58.

SHEA. I do. He's good.

ELIZABETH. And has dealt with these kind of messes before. We're seeing him tomorrow morning.

SHEA. I'm glad to hear that. *(Beat.)* I had to … notify Dartmouth, Lizzy.

ELIZABETH. You — *(This is unexpected.)* you did?

SHEA. If it came out that the school knew and chose *not* to inform them …

ELIZABETH. *(Tight, angry.)* I understand.

SHEA. In any case … Dartmouth's "reconsidering" Brandon's acceptance. *(Beat. This lands hard on Elizabeth, but she's not anywhere near giving up, so:)*

ELIZABETH. Jesus, Jesus Christ!

SHEA. Look it — it could be worse, Liz.

ELIZABETH. Oh? How? How could it be worse?

SHEA. The girl could potentially bring charges against Brandon or the school, but she hasn't yet. Brandon's not yet eighteen, so the news and the papers can't release his name — if it comes to that.

ELIZABETH. They'll … crucify him, Russ, if they can. Even though he is, at heart, a good kid. (I believe that, I *need* to believe that …) Who, essentially, made *one* mistake, it's not that he's like these other — *(Mini-beat.)* the other boys …

SHEA. Which boys, Liz? Are you talking about? *(Beat, then:)*

ELIZABETH. Two months ago, Michael and Brandon were talking about one of Brandon's teammates. Raving about some performance this boy had given in the showers, in the locker room.

SHEA. Performance?

ELIZABETH. Michael explained to me — afterwards, later — that this classmate of Brandon's had brought his girlfriend into the showers after a game, and had sex with her there to, to celebrate the win.

SHEA. In *our* shower room?

ELIZABETH. There was even some kind of — *(Beat.)* After it happened, it was referenced, obliquely, during morning announcements so that the whole school — all the boys, at least — would know it had happened.

SHEA. What I would say to that is: There's talk and there's truth, Lizzy. And the two don't always necessarily overlap.

ELIZABETH. Of course, but we both know St. Joe's has a … history. A … reputation?

SHEA. For what?

ELIZABETH. Oh, come on, Russ. *(Beat.)* Well, for instance, Maddy says — that the St. Joe's boys rate the girls at the girls' schools, one to ten.

SHEA. Didn't you do the same? In your diary, back in high school, which boys were the most handsome? The cutest?

ELIZABETH. They rate them on their ability and willingness to perform oral sex, Russ. Which I certainly did *not* keep track of in my diary. (I didn't even *have* a diary, by the way.)

SHEA. All right —

ELIZABETH. They have contests, Russ — do you know about this? They tell each other which girls will — are *willing* to service them.

SHEA. None of which — I'm sorry, but none of that has anything to do with your son.

ELIZABETH. For me it does. I've been agonizing, trying to think of ways in which what Brandon did could be considered forgivable. And ... there is none, Russ. Except — unless — he were part of a culture that, that glorifies —

SHEA. *(Overlapping.)* Nobody at St. Joseph's is glorifying what Brandon did, Liz, but you want the truth? Yes, it happens. *(Minibeat.)* That behavior? We do our best to control it, reign it in, but they're boys, they're young men, it happens anyway. It's been happening since ... St. Joe's opened its doors. Hell, it happened when Michael and I were students. And the Jesuits back then, when they *really* ran St. Joe's, they were vicious, they didn't care about us. And the lay teachers and the staff, too; we weren't human to them. Transgressions occurred, and people didn't even *bother* to look away. They stared right at them and didn't blink. *(Short pause, then:)* Has Michael ever told you about Andy Monks and Jeff Albertson?

ELIZABETH. I don't think so.

SHEA. They were seniors when Mikey and I were freshmen, and both of them were incredible athletes, Liz — *superlative* athletes, almost exactly evenly matched. And our coach at the time —

ELIZABETH. John Fegan —

SHEA. — he was great with us, the boys, he was everything he should've been, except in this one instance. *(Explaining.)* Fegan couldn't decide who should be captain between Andy and Jeff — and both of them were qualified and wanted it. Both of them had worked for it, and both knew what being captain would mean.

ELIZABETH. *(Unsure what Shea means.)* In the ... St. Joe's hierarchy?

SHEA. And for the rest of their lives, Liz. Something like that — back then more than now, but even now — an *honor* like that ... sets you up a certain way. Prepares you for ... challenges down the line. People start thinking of you a different way, doors start opening, one after the other.

ELIZABETH. How did Fegan end up choosing?

SHEA. He called Andy and Jeff into his office — this same office, as a matter of fact — and told them *they* had to decide. That they had to ... work it out themselves, *then* come to Fegan the next day and tell him who the new captain would be.

ELIZABETH. In other words: Let them kill each other for it.

SHEA. They wrestled — fought — for it. (And we all knew about their contest — students, teachers, *everyone* — but no one tried to stop it.) But they fought ... and Jeff won ... and to prove that he'd won, that he was the better captain, the more powerful man ... So that there wouldn't be any question, he —

ELIZABETH. *(Overlapping, interrupting.)* — *don't.* (Shakes her head.) I don't want to hear, I don't want to hear what that boy did. *(Short pause.)*

SHEA. Afterwards — after Jeff did what he did to Andy — Fegan made Jeff captain, and Andy ... Andy didn't even *play* ... And he was good, as *skilled* a player as Jeff, just not as ...

ELIZABETH. Ruthless. *(Shea shrugs.)* That's — horrific. Incredibly — irresponsible of Fegan.

SHEA. It is — it was — but can I tell you? Things here *have* gotten better, Lizzy. And they'll keep getting better, but on occasion ... a tree doesn't grow the way it should. Doesn't develop properly. It twists and knots ... And it's partly the soil, the — what did you call it?

ELIZABETH. The culture.

SHEA. That's right. But don't delude yourself: It's also the boys, the individual boys who are responsible.

ELIZABETH. Like Jeff Albertson?

SHEA. Yes. *(She goes to one of the pictures in Shea's office.)*

ELIZABETH. I knew *most* of Michael's friends, but I don't remember him ...

SHEA. Well, you wouldn't, like I said, he was older.

ELIZABETH. Russell ... *(Piecing it together slowly, realizing.)* You and Michael were on the football team together...?

SHEA. Every year, side-by-side.

ELIZABETH. Well, except your senior year, when Michael was captain ... *(A short pause.)*

SHEA. That's right, you're right; I broke my arm, just before the season started.

ELIZABETH. How...? *How* did you break your arm? In a fight? *(A beat. Elizabeth's questions seem to be a challenge. Then:)*

SHEA. Do you really want me to answer that, Elizabeth?

ELIZABETH. *(Not accusing, still piecing it together here.)* All this ... Calling me to your office, giving me the tape, not waiting for Michael, who could've made this go away with a phone call ... Because of something Michael did to you? Not Jeff to Andy, Michael to you?

SHEA. I was trying to help Brandon, to help your family.

ELIZABETH. Were you?

SHEA. You can blame me, Liz, you can blame the school, but everything your son's done — every misstep he's taken — that all — belongs — to Brandon. *(This lands on Elizabeth hard.)*

ELIZABETH. I'm fighting for my son's future here. His life, *everything* ...

SHEA. You are. Yes, you are. *(The lights shift and come up on a trail in Rock Creek Park. Justin, wearing track clothes, jogs on. He's been running A LOT — he is sweaty. He stops, bends down, takes deep breaths. A beat, then Brandon steps into view; he'd been waiting for his friend.)*

BRANDON. Justin —

JUSTIN. *(Completely surprised/scared.)* HOLY SHIT!

BRANDON. Sorry. Sorry.

JUSTIN. Jesus, what is your *problem?* What are you *doing* here?

BRANDON. Waiting for you. I know this is where you like to run when — when —

JUSTIN. When I'm in complete psychological turmoil? *(Beat.)* Jesus, I thought you were, like, *Jason.*

BRANDON. Jason?

JUSTIN. Voorhees, from *Friday the 13th.*

BRANDON. I should be at home — my mom thinks I'm at home — but I had to — to —

JUSTIN. *What,* Brandon?

BRANDON. See you? Talk to you?

JUSTIN. Why start now?

BRANDON. What's going on at school, Justin? What are people saying? *(A beat as Justin takes Brandon's question in, then:)*

JUSTIN. *That's* what you want to know? Not — not how *I'm* doing? Not what — Jesus, what *Erica* — what your *girlfriend* — is feeling?

BRANDON. Erica won't — *(Mini-beat.)* I don't think she's talking to me.

JUSTIN. Everyone's shell-shocked; *that's* what's going on. At school? The teachers, the students. Everyone's walking around, across the quad, like — like zombies. It's like — like — like *Dawn of the Dead* meets *A Separate Peace.*

BRANDON. It — it'll pass.

JUSTIN. The whole football team has to perform community service! The entire school has to go on, like, a *three*-day spiritual retreat! There are reporters camped out at the main gate! *(Quick beat.)* We're at Def-Con Four Brandon.

BRANDON. *You* don't have to be. Everyone else can, fuck 'em, but you —

JUSTIN. You *lied* to me! Even though I knew.

BRANDON. You knew what?

JUSTIN. *That it was you on the fucking tape! (Short pause.)* When I begged you to tell me? I was like — ninety-nine-point-nine percent sure it was you.

BRANDON. You barely saw two minutes of it.

JUSTIN. I *have* memorized every part of your body, okay? Every single *cell,* every single *follicle.*

BRANDON. Don't, Justin. Don't say shit like that.

JUSTIN. Why, it makes you *uncomfortable?*

BRANDON. *(Not going there.)* If you were so sure, why didn't you tell me?

JUSTIN. Wow, are you *truly* that dense? *(Beat.)* I wanted *you* to tell me. To my face.

BRANDON. I'm telling you now, to your face.

JUSTIN. Too fucking late! You've — you've wrecked it, Brandon! People — people are calling you a rapist.

BRANDON. This'll — this'll blow over. It's a — a bump.

JUSTIN. A bump? Brandon, you are going to be expelled for what you did to Cheryl Moody! *(Beat.)* Father Lawton and Coach Shea? Yeah, your dad's friends with the Coach, yeah, they're pals, but they are going to *slaughter* you. What did you say? "Make an example of one — then bury the rest of it"? That's what they're going to do — *to you. (Furious at Brandon, at himself.)* Christ, all because of that stupid, *stupid* night at the pool.

BRANDON. Don't start that bullshit again!

JUSTIN. That night, that *fateful* night at the Varsity pool, when Mitchell came in —

BRANDON. We weren't *doing* anything —

JUSTIN. We were *naked,* Brandon —

BRANDON. So?

40

JUSTIN. So Mitchell came in —

BRANDON. Yeah, Mitchell came in and *what?* We were talking —

JUSTIN. I was jacking you off —

BRANDON. I'm not even sure Mitchell saw that. The pool was dark, we were in the water, and he was — I mean, he was *completely* drunk. Like he always is.

JUSTIN. Why his locker, then, huh? Out of four hundred lockers?

BRANDON. He — he leaves it unlocked!

JUSTIN. Please, Brandon, I'm not a fucking douche bag! *(Beat.)* Christ, what did you imagine? One scandal — a better scandal — replacing another? So no one starts thinking you're —

BRANDON. *(Overlapping.)* I'm not gay —

JUSTIN. *(Overlapping.)* Yes, you are, and oh, look — the world still's turning! Nobody at school cares about me —

BRANDON. Yeah, they *do* care, you just have no clue what they *really* think about you. What they call you behind your back.

JUSTIN. Yeah, I know, cocksucker, who — ?

BRANDON. *(Vicious and ugly.)* Yeah, and *shiteater. (Beat.)* And *cumboy. (Beat.)* And AIDS *faggot. (Beat.)* You wanna hear more? They *know,* Justin. That you suck my cock? They know, and can I tell you what they say, what they ask me? "Would he do me, too?" "Would he suck both of us, together, at the same time, if we asked him?" *(A beat — Justin takes this in — then:)*

JUSTIN. God, what kills me…? Is that when we started talking in the locker room — on the first day of our freshman year — and I recognized something in you, and you recognized something in me —

BRANDON. I didn't —

JUSTIN. *(Overlapping.)* You *did* — *(Beat.)* I saw it all, how this all played out, I thought: "This is going to end badly."

BRANDON. I'm sorry, Justin, you thought that.

JUSTIN. You deserve everything that's coming to you!

BRANDON. Fuck you —

JUSTIN. *(Overlapping.)* And maybe, hopefully, it'll actually *do* something to you. It'll maybe get you to admit —

BRANDON. JUSTIN —

JUSTIN. WHAT?

BRANDON. Did you tell Shea? *(Beat.)* Where to find Cheryl Moody? *(Beat.)* We've been to that mall together …

JUSTIN. You think *I* told Shea…? You think *I* was the one…?

BRANDON. Justin — *answer the fucking question!* — were you?

41

(Justin thinks about it, then:)

JUSTIN. This is what I have to say to that: You're *not* gay … and I *didn't* tell Shea. *(A beat, then:)*

BRANDON. If I kicked the shit out of you, would you answer me, then?

JUSTIN. Go ahead. *(He opens his arms, wide.)* Do it, beat me to a pulp. *(Brandon doesn't move.)* DO IT! Come on, I know you're not *scared* to, I know you get off on shit like that! *(A beat. We should think that maybe Brandon will do something physical here for a few moments, but … he doesn't. Instead, he turns away, scowling.)*

BRANDON. You're not worth it.

JUSTIN. Or anything, apparently.

BRANDON. Even if I *get* expelled, even if I *don't* go to Dartmouth —

JUSTIN. You will be, and you won't —

BRANDON. — I'll still go *further* than you. Make *more* money than you. Be happier than you. Have a better *life* than you.

JUSTIN. Never talk to me again! Never call me. Never seek me out. If we see each other — anywhere — on the street — in passing — don't stop, don't say hi, don't wave, don't *anything*. We're *strangers*. We mean *nothing* to each other. *(The lights shift, Justin goes one way, Brandon goes the other, and we find ourselves in the food court at Montgomery Mall, where Cheryl sits at a table, doing some homework. After a few moments, Elizabeth enters. She sees Cheryl, approaches her tentatively, stops, stares at the girl. Who eventually looks up.)*

CHERYL. I'm on my break, ma'am, so if there's a problem …

ELIZABETH. No, no problem. *(Unsure all of a sudden.)* Is that — homework you're doing?

CHERYL. Extra credit. For Spanish.

ELIZABETH. My, my sister teaches Spanish.

CHERYL. Uhm…?

ELIZABETH. You're Cheryl Moody, aren't you?

CHERYL. Yes, but I'm not talking —

ELIZABETH. Cheryl, I'm Elizabeth Hardy. *(No reaction from Cheryl.)* Brandon's mother?

CHERYL. … Oh.

ELIZABETH. Could I — ? Could I sit — ?

CHERYL. You can — *(Elizabeth does, she joins Cheryl.)* — but I don't have anything to say to you, ma'am.

ELIZABETH. You don't have to call me "ma'am."

CHERYL. Mrs. Hardy.

ELIZABETH. You can call me "Elizabeth."

CHERYL. I probably shouldn't call you *anything* — I mean, right?

ELIZABETH. Right ... I am so ... *outraged* for you — I want you to know. *(Beat.)* Of all the things Brandon did, what outrages me most is that he did these things ... to you. Someone ... *(Searching for the phrase.)* outside his circle. That he brought you down the way he did, it just ... *outrages* me.

CHERYL. Outrages ... *you?*

ELIZABETH. I — I realize my saying that probably doesn't *mean* much.

CHERYL. It doesn't mean *anything,* 'cause everyone knows what happened, Mrs. Hardy. In my life? In my *"circle?"* Everyone. I mean, my mother and *father* know, they *saw* what I did.

ELIZABETH. They — they've watched the tape?

CHERYL. *Everyone's* watched the tape, Mrs. Hardy — haven't you?

ELIZABETH. Yes.

CHERYL. Awful, right?

ELIZABETH. Yes. *(The horror of it:)* Your mother and father ...

CHERYL. Want to kill your son — slooooooowly ...

ELIZABETH. *(Not looking at her.)* And you? Do *you* want to kill Brandon?

CHERYL. I ... *(Thinks about it.)* I was so *pissed* when Jeanine — she's one of my friends — when she told me what everyone was saying, what he'd done. I was so pissed, I drove to St. Joe's — with my friends — to, like, confront him, and yell at him, and make him face me.

ELIZABETH. Brandon didn't tell me that.

CHERYL. He doesn't know. *(Beat.)* When we saw him, he was walking with this other guy, and Jeanine was like: "Now, go now, tear him a new one." And I wanted to, I did — I *thought* I did ... I mean, he tricked me, and humiliated me, and pretty much ruined my life, but what does that say about him? How messed up must *he* be?

ELIZABETH. ... Very. *(She nods.)* Very.

CHERYL. God, if I could rewind and *not* go with your son —

ELIZABETH. Why *did* you?

CHERYL. *(Sharply.)* Excuse me?

ELIZABETH. No, I'm not judging you, I only ...

CHERYL. Want someone to blame?

ELIZABETH. No. *(Mini-beat.)* Yes. *(Mini-beat.)* I'm trying to understand ...

CHERYL. What would make anyone, after only one conversation…?

ELIZABETH. Do that — yes.

CHERYL. Mrs. Hardy … have you *seen* your son? Do you *realize* what he looks like?

ELIZABETH. He's … handsome.

CHERYL. *(Correcting her.)* He's *foxy* — the *foxiest.* And the things he said to me? I'd been waiting for someone like your son to say those things to me since sixth grade. *(Quick beat.)* On *top* of which … you went to Garrison, right?

ELIZABETH. I did.

CHERYL. And you're a doctor?

ELIZABETH. Yes …

CHERYL. And your husband, he's a doctor, too?

ELIZABETH. He is.

CHERYL. Okay, well …

ELIZABETH. I'm sorry, I don't …

CHERYL. You're over there, Mrs. Hardy — on that side of the table — and I'm over here, on *this* side, and … it's gonna take me awhile to get over there. *(Beat.)* Oh, I'm gonna do it — I'm *doing* it — it's not like it's impossible, it's not like I'm *homeless* — but it's not gonna be super easy or super fun. Getting over to where you and Brandon are — live.

ELIZABETH. Right — yes.

CHERYL. When your son asked me to go out with him, I — I had this fantasy for a second. Like maybe we would start dating, and go to the same college, and get married, and — and — and maybe my life would be easier than I think it's gonna be, you know? Maybe I could be *that* girl — I thought. Fantasized. *(Shrugs.)* Stupid, but I did …

ELIZABETH. It's not stupid. It's — it's what we all do … *(Elizabeth builds to this question.)* Cheryl, did my son…? Did Brandon, when you were with him…? Did he…? Did he force you? *(A beat.)*

CHERYL. I'm not sure *what* it was … I know that when he started to kiss me in his car, I *liked* it, I *liked* that he was kissing me … And I know that when he told me he had to check on this house for a friend, as a favor, 'cause they were away, I wanted to laugh, because it was just so ridiculous, so obviously …

ELIZABETH. A lie.

CHERYL. Did you see the whole tape, from beginning to end?

ELIZABETH. Yes.

CHERYL. Okay, well, you can't hear it, but right when we started, I heard him, like, whimpering?

ELIZABETH. He was?

CHERYL. I asked if he was okay, and ... he was, he said, but *that's* when it got ...

ELIZABETH. *(Hoping "intense" is all it got.)* Intense?

CHERYL. *(Carefully, sparing Liz.)* ... sure. *(Beat.)* But it was kind of too late, you know, by then?

ELIZABETH. I truly ... *truly* hate that you were dragged into this. *(Beat.)* If there's anything I can do ... *(Cheryl just looks at Elizabeth for a beat or two, then says:)*

CHERYL. You know, people say that — "If there's anything I can do" — but do they mean it?

ELIZABETH. I do.

CHERYL. As in, like, reparations? For damages inflicted upon me by your son?

ELIZABETH. Uhhhh ...

CHERYL. Hey, yeah. Like you could maybe give me an allowance so I could take one night off per week? That way — at least — I'd have a weekly break from people gawking at the — at the *whore.*

ELIZABETH. The...?

CHERYL. And I could study some more — get a little bit ahead? Catch up to the AP kids because my school doesn't have AP classes?

ELIZABETH. I ...

CHERYL. Or — if you *really* want to make up for the tape — maybe you could agree to subsidize my college education? In case my scholarships don't come through? ('Cause let's face it; no one's gonna give a whore like me an academic scholarship.)

ELIZABETH. Don't call yourself that. You're not a —

CHERYL. I mean, there actually *is* something you could do — a *lot* you could do. *(Beat.)* If you wanted to.

ELIZABETH. I do —

CHERYL. You don't — *(Mini-beat.)* but you like *thinking* you're the kind of person who does. *(Cheryl stands to go.)* It seems like to me. *(Cheryl exits, the lights shift, come up on the living room, where Brandon sits, on the couch, watching TV. He turns it off when Elizabeth crosses to him.)*

BRANDON. *(Almost accusingly.)* They showed St Joe's on the news. The school, the campus. There was this reporter, standing in the quad, in front of the gym, talking about the tape, and the football team, saying things like — like — *(Quick beat.)* these *lies* about us! Making shit up about — about *rituals* — and *hazing* — and — and — *God, just bullshit!*

ELIZABETH. Were you — did they mention you by name?

BRANDON. No, but — *tonight* was the first of a series, he said, about what goes on at St. Joe's, so stay tuned for the true story.

ELIZABETH. *(Quietly, to herself.)* "Behind Ivy-Covered Walls … "

BRANDON. Where *were* you, mom?

ELIZABETH. I went to see Russell … then I went to Montgomery Mall … then to Garrison … and walked around there for … hours, looking at the girls, trying to remember what it was like … what *I* was like …

BRANDON. You, you went to the mall?

ELIZABETH. I did. I talked to the girl; I talked to *Cheryl.*

BRANDON. Was that a, a good idea?

ELIZABETH. She's tough, isn't she…? *(Quickest beat.)* And smart, too. I *liked* that; I hope it means she's going to survive this.

BRANDON. She will. We all will.

ELIZABETH. She reminded me of a girl from Garrison, whose name was … This is ancient history now, but it was Alice, Alice Kinney … *(She looks at him.)* Alice transferred in our junior year, she wasn't someone we'd grown up with, which made it more difficult for her to, to acclimate. And she so desperately wanted to be in, to be one of us … And the way she decided she was going to do that was to land a boy, the *right* kind of boyfriend. From St. Joseph's, or Gonzaga, or Landon, or — really, it had to be one of those three.

BRANDON. Same thing now.

ELIZABETH. Is it? Landon's still in the mix?

BRANDON. Yeah, you're supposed to —

ELIZABETH. — right; you're "*supposed* to." *(Beat.)* Our junior year, there was a party, at a boy's house, from St. Joseph's — *(Asking him.)* — and the host of this party *was…?*

BRANDON. … Dad?

ELIZABETH. Your father, yes. Who asked me to invite Alice, which I thought was incredibly … *generous* of him … And I planned to keep track of her, throughout the night, but Alice seemed to be doing fine, and I was … with your dad. So I, more or less, forgot about her … Until around midnight, when your dad and I were in a gazebo, in front of his house, talking — (and we *were* just talking) — and one of his friends came up to us, and said, "It's happening, right now, hurry!" And your dad, he leapt up, and ran off with this boy — and this other boy was ... Russell.

BRANDON. Where'd they go? When they ran off?

ELIZABETH. Around the house, to the back of the house — I followed them — and they were all there ... Your father, Russ, their teammates ... And one of them was up on a ladder that had been set against the house, and he was ... peering into a window, on the second floor.

BRANDON. A ladder?

ELIZABETH. Your father and his friends had organized a windowsill party ... Those don't exist anymore, do they?

BRANDON. I ... don't know what they are.

ELIZABETH. Inside that room, Brandon? On the second floor? Alice Kinney was losing her virginity to a boy from St. Joe's, and the boy's friends — your father, included — were taking turns, watching them ... I stood there; I saw them climb up and down that ladder, one by one ... *(Beat.)* And it had been *planned* ... And I had *participated* ...

BRANDON. Yeah, but — unknowingly.

ELIZABETH. *(Shaking her head.)* No, I knew ... I knew something ... *(Beat.)* I had an idea, when your dad asked me to invite Alice, of what was coming ... And part of me, when I *really* look back on it, when I really force myself to, Brandon ... Part of me *consented* to it happening ... *(Almost rationalizing.)* If it happened to Alice, and if she became dirty, or damaged, or spoiled — and she did, she left mid-term, we were cruel to her after that night — but if our boyfriends did what they wanted to Alice, then maybe they wouldn't do it us ...

BRANDON. Jesus ...

ELIZABETH. That's what they did, what they were going to do, to someone, and ... better her than us.

BRANDON. Mom, Jesus ... *(He starts towards her; she stops him with:)*

ELIZABETH. I'm ready now, I think, for all of it, everything. I'm ready for you to say it. *(Beat.)* Do you realize — and *accept* — and *own* — that you did something horrible — beyond horrible — to Cheryl Moody? The way your father and his friends did — and I did — to Alice Kinney?

BRANDON. Of, of course.

ELIZABETH. What? What did you do?

BRANDON. I lied to her …

ELIZABETH. Yes. What else?

BRANDON. And … used her …

ELIZABETH. You did. What else?

BRANDON. And didn't care about her, her feelings …

ELIZABETH. You treated her like she was a *thing* — like she was nothing.

BRANDON. Mom …

ELIZABETH. *That's* what you did, that's what you have to take responsibility for. And not just for a week, not just for a semester, for the *rest of your life.* You're going to carry this — *I'm* going to make sure you carry this — for as long as Cheryl Moody has to.

BRANDON. Fine, I — I'm ready for that.

ELIZABETH. No, not yet, but you will be —

BRANDON. — OK.

ELIZABETH. And you keep saying it, but do you feel remorse for what you did? You break your ribs open before you answer me!

BRANDON. Break my — ?

ELIZABETH. That's what we do — to get to someone's heart in surgery — we break their ribs open and we pry them back.

BRANDON. I *am* sorry, mom —

ELIZABETH. Careful: That would mean you have a conscience. That would mean you know right from wrong. That would mean no more shirking —

BRANDON. I'm not.

ELIZABETH. Then you have to make me understand why — not how, *why* — you did what you did.

BRANDON. I told you: I don't know.

ELIZABETH. No. Not good enough, not *nearly* — *(Quickest beat.)* Why did you show your friends the tape? *(Nothing from him. Then:)* Brandon —

BRANDON. We, we all show each other —

ELIZABETH. What?

BRANDON. What we *do.* It's like a *game* —

ELIZABETH. What you can get away with? (Oh, God …) Under our noses?

BRANDON. It is no big deal, mom.

ELIZABETH. But it *is*, Brandon, it is a big deal.

BRANDON. I didn't think it would turn into anything.

ELIZABETH. You didn't think there would be consequences? You thought — what, even if you were caught — you thought St. Joe's would, would protect you?

BRANDON. Yeah — yes — a little bit. *(A beat. Elizabeth takes this in.)*

ELIZABETH. All right, but why Cheryl? Why with her? Why the way you did it? *(Beat.)* Did something happen with Erica? Were you angry at her and — ?

BRANDON. What? No, she — she's great, we're gonna get over this, we're gonna get married.

ELIZABETH. Oh, Brandon, do you really believe that? *(A long, clear beat. A decision to ask:)* Look at me. Was it because of Justin? Your friendship with Justin?

BRANDON. My "friendship" …? *(Elizabeth has to make a choice: Is this all going to come out…? Yes …)*

ELIZABETH. You don't have to lie, I don't care, just tell me — is it because of Justin?

BRANDON. No. It had *nothing* to do with that faggot.

ELIZABETH. Don't. He is *not* that word.

BRANDON. He is, Mom, he's *disgusting.*

ELIZABETH. If it's not about Erica, and it's not about Justin —

BRANDON. I wanted …

ELIZABETH. What? What did you want?

BRANDON. *(Strong, sudden.) I wanted to do it!*

ELIZABETH. Why?

BRANDON. I wanted to feel what it would be like to — to —

ELIZABETH. *Tell me!*

BRANDON. I DON'T KNOW! *(Unraveling.)* Something happened, mom … Inside me … Something happened, and I *thought* I could hurt her … Make her feel scared …

ELIZABETH. *(Horrified by this admission.) Why?* Why did you think that?

BRANDON. Because … she doesn't … *matter* …

ELIZABETH. She *does,* though … Look at me. *(He does.)* She *does* matter … *More* than you … *More* than me …

BRANDON. We'll fix this, we can fix this … when Dad gets here …

ELIZABETH. Just like that? A call to Father Lawton, and all this goes away? All the bowling pins stand back up?

BRANDON. Yeah — *(Nodding.)* yes …

ELIZABETH. No, Brandon, no … Everything is broken; not just this one thing, *everything* … *(Listing them.)* Cheryl; her parents;

49

Erica; Maddy; Justin; your father; me; our house; our family; our name; *everything* ... Broken, even if Cheryl and her family decide *not* to, to *decimate* you — and they should; *I* would, if she were my daughter ... I would *hound* you, I wouldn't stop until there was *nothing* left ...

BRANDON. Why? It wasn't that bad —

ELIZABETH. It was. You don't understand ... You have *no* idea ... (You've never answered for anything; *we've* never made you answer for anything ...) *(Beat.)* But *I* can tell you what's coming; some of it, at least ...

BRANDON. You don't have to, Mom —

ELIZABETH. Yes, I *do. (Beat.)* Dartmouth? (And believe me, this is the least of it.) But Dartmouth? Whatever that was going to be for you — that's gone now.

BRANDON. Not, not necessarily ...

ELIZABETH. Yes. *Yes,* necessarily ... *(Beat. More.)* And I'm sorry but you're done at St. Joseph's.

BRANDON. NO —

ELIZABETH. Yes, Brandon, even if the suspension *doesn't* turn into an expulsion — even if your father ... *Whatever* he threatens ... you are *done* at that school.

BRANDON. *WHY,* Mom? Are you doing this?

ELIZABETH. To help you. I'm trying to help you. I *love* you ... And I promised I would stand by your side, no matter what, and I will ... I am ... Whatever you did, I *don't* believe you're all the things they're going to call you ... (And they will; prepare yourself for that; prepare to be called a, a rapist — a degenerate — a sociopath — a monster.)

BRANDON. I'm not — You know me —

ELIZABETH. I don't, Brandon, I don't ... *(Short pause.)* You're ... confused, you are *so* confused ... And you did a terrible, a *horrific* thing, but I don't think you're beyond ... *(Unsaid: " ... saving ... ")* I believe — I *hope* ... You may not be able to atone for what you've done — and we, your father and I — we may not be able to atone for what we've done —

BRANDON. Nothing. You guys didn't do anything.

ELIZABETH. Oh, we *made* you — this life — built it together — we *let* this happen ... *(Amending; the truth.)* I let this happen ...

BRANDON. You did?

ELIZABETH. *(Nodding, one last memory.)* When your father

asked me to marry him, we were at a dance, a cotillion, downtown, at the Willard, so elegant … It was after the night with Alice Kinney, but I *still* wanted him … (He was so handsome, in his coat and tie …) And he chose me … and *I* chose him … and there was an *understanding* between us …

BRANDON. What? *(She turns from him.)*

ELIZABETH. This house … When we first walked into this house — (there was nothing, it was empty, it was *new* …) we passed from room to room, and I wasn't sure, but your dad kept saying, "You will be happy here, you will be happy here … "

BRANDON. *(At an utter loss.)* I don't understand what's wrong …

ELIZABETH. You will — I promise you. *(They are looking at each other, this mother and son, barely recognizing each other. The lights on them fade … and come up on Justin, in the locker room, at his lockers. Brandon crosses to join him. They look younger somehow. Like freshmen. They're changing into their P.E. uniforms.)*

JUSTIN. Excuse me, do we — ? *(Brandon looks at him.)* Hi — sorry — do you know if these are gonna be our lockers for, like, the next four years?

BRANDON. No, this is — just when we're freshmen. Next year, we'll be on the — on the other side of the weight room.

JUSTIN. Right. *(They continue changing in silence for a few moments. Then:)*

BRANDON. You playing football?

JUSTIN. At least — this year, at least. I mean, all the freshmen are "strongly encouraged to," right? Wasn't that in our welcome packet?

BRANDON. My dad says that some of the guys he met playing football at St. Joe's are still some of his closest friends.

JUSTIN. Your father went here?

BRANDON. He did. Class of Fifty … something. Did your dad go here?

JUSTIN. No, I'm — I'm the first one in my family.

BRANDON. Lucky. *(Extending his hand.)* I'm Brandon, Brandon Hardy.

JUSTIN. Justin Simmons. *(They shake.)* You're lucky you're not a Frank or a Joe.

BRANDON. A…?

JUSTIN. As in the Hardy Boys, as in Frank and Joe Hardy?

BRANDON. Oh — right.

JUSTIN. I've read every single book, like, *twice.*

BRANDON. You have?

JUSTIN. I guess I kind of have a soft spot for those v-neck sweaters they're always wearing. *(Brandon doesn't know what to say.)* Sorry. Sorry, that's just lame.

BRANDON. No, it's funny. You're — funny.

JUSTIN. Uhm … thanks.

BRANDON. Hey, if you want — in class — when we split into teams? If you want, we could be on the same team.

JUSTIN. Sure.

BRANDON. Hey — "The Tower Treasure."

JUSTIN. Huh?

BRANDON. "The Tower Treasure." That's the first Hardy Boys book — adventure. (You call yourself a fan?) It goes "The Tower Treasure," then "The House on the Cliff" —

JUSTIN. Oh, my God, followed by —

BRANDON and JUSTIN. "The Secret of the Old Mill" —

JUSTIN. — oh, my God!

BRANDON. This, incidentally, is the last conversation we're having about the Hardy Boys in public, okay?

JUSTIN. Okay.

BRANDON. You swear?

JUSTIN. I swear — Jesus!

BRANDON. Good. *(Brandon smiles at Justin, who smiles back. The lights on them fade as they continue changing clothes …)*

End of Play

PROPERTY LIST

Miscellaneous sports equipment
VCR
Videotape
TV
Large sports bag
Whistle
Beeper
Baseball
Soda and fries
2 cups of coffee
Homework

SOUND EFFECTS

Door opening and closing
Ring of a school bell